GW00634573

"NA

POLITICALLY I   E

Written by SCULLION

Drawings by RICHARD KINGSTON

~~oOo~~

This book is published by **Bunford Press**, The Estate Office, Little Brympton, Yeovil, Somerset.

Every effort has been used to avoid the use of Trademarks. The presence of a word in this publication, whether marked or unmarked, in no way affects its legal status as a Trademark.

First published by **Bunford Press** – 2005.

ISBN: 0-9507124-5-0

Copyright **Bunford Press** – 2005. This publication is copyright in all countries which are signatories to the Berne Convention.

All rights reserved. No part of this publication may be reproduced, stored in a retrieval system, nor transmitted by any means electronic, mechanical, photocopying or otherwise without the prior permission of the publisher. The right of Scullion is to be identified as the author of this publication and has been asserted by him in accordance with the Copyright, Design and Patents Acts, 1988.

All characters, people and names in this publication are fictional. Resemblance to any person, living or dead, or any place, here or abroad, is pure co-incidence.

Bath Night is on the first Friday of every month.

~oOo~

Bunford Press
www.bunfordpress.com

"NAUGHTY!"

POLITICALLY INCORRECT NURSERY VERSE

Written by SCULLION

Drawings by RICHARD KINGSTON

~~oOo~~

Published by Bunford Press
www.bunfordpress.com

To Whom it May Concern

Regardless of your clan, claque, clone, class, club, clique or
cluster, no deep offence has been intended.
I hope that none will be taken.

The contents of this book have been shamelessly plundered
from the originality and genius of Belloc, Betjeman, Carrol,
Gilbert, Lear, *et al*; but especially from that most prolific of
all versifiers – Anon.

I offer them by grateful thanks – and humble apologies!

Scullion

INTRODUCTION

Thomas Jefferson   *4thJuly 1776*

(The Declaration of Independence)

"All men are created equal. They are endowed by their Creator with certain unalienable rights, that among these are Life, Liberty and the Pursuit of Happiness."

Scullion   *4thJuly 2005*

(A Declaration in the Pub)

"......... you must be joking, Mate!"

~~oOo~~

CONTENTS

THE PURSUIT OF HAPPINESS...

LIFE ...

Jack and Jill

Jack chased Jill
Right up the hill
And, at the top,
He caught her!

Jill came down,
With half a crown,
For 'naughty' games
He taught her!

~~oOo~~

Pat-a-cake

Pat-a-cake, pat-a-cake; call it a flan.

Mixing preservatives, in with the bran.

List all the additives, known unto man.

Call it 'ORGANIC', whenever you can!

~~oOo~~

Here's the Church

Here's the church.
Here's the steeple.
Open the door
And where's the people?

Nobody bothering,
Nobody cares.
And nobody quietly
Saying their prayers.

~~oOo~~

The Environmental Health Officer

I'm terribly keen on my Saint.
In fact, I think him a star.
Some say that his habits are quaint;
I like them, the way that they are.

I then saw St. George – in a van!
I feared that his horse might be lame;
Or worse, in a Kennomeat can,
When hurt in some chivalric game.

He told me, "I'm not very happy,
Now carried around, in this way.
I used to dress well and quite snappy,
With armour and sword, on display."

It didn't seem right, when I saw him
In wellies and uniformed hat.
I hoped that my Saint would look trim
And not like some grim bureaucrat.

He told me, "I'm here on a mission.
I think it's called 'vermin control.'
Without any Council Permission
There's something shacked up – in a hole!"

"You there," said St. George to a swain,
"I need you to help, with my quest.
They're wanting this Dragon thing slain.
I'm told it's becoming a pest."

"Noble Saint, may it please you to hark,
'Tis Ramblers and Naturalists Day.
They're swarming all over the Park,
Demanding a new Right of Way!"

"Yon Dragon is hid in a cave
And hiding away, from the masses.
He claims he's no longer so brave,
When facing unlawful trespassers."

The Saint then drove off in his banger,
But soon got it stuck in the mud.
He then was assailed by the clamour
Of city folk, baying for blood.

Just then, he received a surprise,
When ordered to purchase a ticket;
For watching 'A Dragon which cries
And cowers, behind a small thicket.'

St. George next fastened his tabard
(Bio-degradable tin!)
And drew out his sword, from its scabbard.
He gingerly ventured within.

"Brave Saint, you have come and will save me,
Before I am forced back to crime;
Or those ghastly do-gooders enslave me.
Thank God that you've got here, in time."

"I've finished with Dragonly trades.
My fire blasting days have all ceased.
I love little children and maids.
I'm now't but a terrified beast."

St. George said, "My job must be done.
This isn't the world, as we knew it.
The Chivalry era is run."
He took out his sword – and he slew it!

~~oOo~~

My Mother Said

My mother said
I never should
Play with the gypsies,
In the wood.

If I did,
She would say;
"Immigrants!
They must not stay!"

Georgy Porgy

Georgy Porgy, pudding and pie,
Kissed the girls. It made him cry.
When the boys came out to play,
Georgy Porgy squeaked "I'm gay!"

~~oOo~~

Youth

When I'm old, I am sure I'll be grey;
Retirement, a long holiday.
But now, as a lad,
Life's boring and sad,
When scrabbling about for some pay.

In future, I hope to be wise;
With mind of a generous size.
But now, I just grunt,
My attitudes blunt,
Which others all hate and despise.

In time, I will happiness spread;
Be seen as a wise figurehead.
But me? I am tired.
I'm seldom inspired
And have to be dragged from my bed.

I am sure female hearts will compete;
As they swoon, by the score, at my feet.
But now, pulling birds,
I stumble for words.
They scatter, in hasty retreat.

When I'm old, I will pray people say
I'm fun, if invited to stay.
But now people moan
Or scream down the phone.
I **DO** wish they'd all go away!

~~oOo~~

Old Age

In my youth, I am sure, I was slim.
A waist line, both modest and trim.
But now that I'm old,
So frequently told,
My features are wrinkled and grim.

As a lad, to be agile and quick;
At games, always stylish and slick;
But all of it's gone.
I just hobble on,
Alone, with a stout walking stick.

I think I had girls by the score;
Unlimited pussy galore.
No more sex appeal,
Instead they all reel
And claim I'm a lecherous bore.

In my prime, I would argue, roughshod.
Demosthenes, then, was my God.
But now, I just drone;
I mumble and groan
And gripe, like a grumpy old sod.

Every day, I just look at the walls.
The time, on the mantelpiece, crawls.
But is that a knock,
A turn of the lock?
I **DO** hope that somebody calls!

~~oOo~~

Humpty Dumpty

Humpty Dumpty sat on a wall.
Humpty Dumpty had a great fall.

With floods of Directives, from the EU.
To put him together – they hadn't a clue!

~~oOo~~

The Grand Old Duke of York

The Grand Old Duke of York,
He had a thousand men.
The Pay Review then checked his staff
And cut him down to ten!

They took his tank; the armoured car,
Some rifles and a Bren.
And then they said he couldn't have
His pretty little Wren.
The grand old Duke of York
Once had a thousand men.
They've stripped the lot. There's nothing left!
They even took his pen!

~~oOo~~

Rock-a-bye-Baby

Rock-a-bye baby
In the tree top.
When the wind blows
The cradle will rock.
When the bough breaks,
The cradle will fall.
Then down will come baby
And cradle and all!

What hope has the baby,
Stuck up in a tree?
A mighty odd place,
Between you and me.
And when the wind blows,
I'm sure you'll agree,
It's BOUND to come down,
You thick dungaree!

~~oOo~~

If You Go Down ...

If you go down to the woods today,
You'll hope for a quiet surprise.
There's nothing like watching young animals play,
With which you can empathize.

But anoraks, now, are everywhere;
Thrashing and crashing around.
Or sanctimonious volunteers,
On a 'feel good' merry-go-round.

If you slip down to the woods today,
There won't be a quiet surprise.
Today it's filled with greenies, who
Just shout – and criticize!

~~oOo~~

Tower of Babel

I want to take you to a place
where grown-ups like to play.
They come in haste, to state their case;
then bicker night and day.
A world of gross insanity;
of mirrors, tricks and lights.
That palace of inanity,
The Court of Human Rights.

Now if you've got a little gripe,
some niggle or a wheeze;
Are you the type, who wants to swipe
when someone fails to please?
Don't waste your time in prudency.
Go climb the dizzy heights
And try that place of lunacy,
The Court of Human Rights.

~~oOo~~

Mary

"Mary, Mary, quite contrary.
Your garden's a splendid show.
How do you get such massive crops,
I really want to know?"

"With pesticides, insecticides
And chemicals, all in a row.
I raise two fingers to all the 'Greens',
Then watch my treasures grow!"

~~oOo~~

Bobby Shafto

Bobby Shafto went to sea,
With silver buckles on his knee.
He's not the sort to marry me;
With sailors, he would rather be.

Bobby Shafto's looks were fair;
He loved to comb his dyed blond hair.
Dark leather clad his *derrière*.
You saw his picture everywhere.

Bobby Shafto's tall and slim;
He always dressed so neat and trim.
The ladies all just gazed at him
And thought, "Oh what a cherubim!"

Bobby Shafto's left the scene;
On telly he's no longer seen;
Except in ads for margarine,
Or hanging out in Golders Green!

~~oOo~~

Legacy

My Father died, a month ago,
And left me all his money.
But since he had an overdraft,
I didn't find it funny.

His Brother got the cheque book stubs;
My Mum, a garden spade.
To Sis, the apple of his eye,
He left his hearing aid!

~~oOo~~

Baa! Baa! Black Sheep

Baa! Baa! .... (whoopsie!) sheep.
Mustn't use that word!
And who the hell's to say I can't,
When insult's not inferred?
To stifle speech is surely wrong
In fact, it's quite absurd!

~~oOo~~

Oh Dear!

Oh dear! What can the matter be?
Johnny stopped by. He cuddled and patted me;
Busied himself about my anatomy.
Now he's shoved off to the Fair!

Oh dear! What can the matter be?
Morning sickness, a bit of a drat-a-by.
Every day my waistline gets fat-a-by.
Johnny's away at the Fair!

Oh dear! What can the matter be?
Social Service has set out to 'rescue' me;
Saying I'm clever, with oodles of flattery.
Johnny's still doing the Fair!

Oh dear! What can the matter be?
Now I've got a wee pitt-a-pattery.
Safely installed in my new little flat, you see,
Johnny's come back from the Fair!

~~oOo~~

N.H.S.

Away! Away!
Without delay,
In hospital,
To spend the day

And there you'll sit
And wait and stay.
So what! It's free?

It's not! You pay!

~~oOo~~

Hickory Dickory Dock

Hickory Dickory Dock.
A mouse ran up the clock.
Its digital face,
To him, was a case
Of utter poppycock!

~~oOo~~

No More Fish Knives

Do 'phone for a Pizza, dear Norman,
Since Olga is having a strop.
Then say that we want it delivered.
I'm not going down to the shop.

I must send a text to Jemima.
We may get an e-mail from Max
And, whilst you're still by the computer,
Do put some more bumph in the fax.

Tonight is that Charity Auction;
Clarissa said come as we are.
And bring along lots of spondooleys;
They charge us a bomb, at the Bar!

We'll have to get Desmond to call in.
The sauna is starting to leak.
My microwave's out of commission
And Henry's beginning to squeak.

Now give me some thoughts for our Party,
The one at the end of the week.
It's got to be terribly ethnic.
All ouzo and feta and Greek.

I want to have proper Moussaka;
Souvlaki, that's straight from the grill.
Oregano and fresh coriander,
All drizzled about with some dill.

Oh, Norman! For God's sake kick Olga.
She's getting me rather un-nerved.
And tell her to un-wrap the Pizza.
I do want it daintily served!

~~oOo~~

It's Raining

It's raining!
It's pouring!
I wish that I was snoring.

With quite a head,
I went to bed
And now, it's bloody morning!

~~oOo~~

Dumbing Down

There was a king, as I've been told,
Who ruled the land, in days of old.
Although he wore a Crown of gold,
His heart was sound and just.

He hated tales, that someone poor,
Could never enter through the door
Reserved for Peers, with breeding pure.
It filled him with disgust.

"It is" he said, "a just reward,
Of Human Rights, to be a Lord.
Not kept for those, with acres broad
And from the upper crust."

And when they came, from 'round the globe,
He dubbed them all, with Royal Probe.
And so the treasured ermine robe
Was worth no more than dust!

~~oOo~~

Little Jack Horner

Fatty-boy Horner
Sits in the corner,
Eating a microwaved pie.

He's just eaten eight,
Is now overweight.
Nutritionalists say he will die!

~~oOo~~

The Wise Old Owl

The wise old owl lived in an oak.
The more he heard, the less he spoke.

In fact, the bird is pretty dumb
And near extinction, now become!

~~oOo~~

Doctor Foster

Doctor Foster
Went to Gloucester;
Abortion was his game.

What Cupid hid,
He soon undid
And mighty rich became!

~~oOo~~

LIBERTY .....

Hey Diddle Diddle

Hey diddle diddle,
The Cat's on the fiddle
And claiming his Benefit dole!

He hops on a 'plane,
(His Villa's in Spain,)
Then lives off the moolah he stole!

~~oOo~~

One Two

One two three four five,
Once I caught a thief, alive.
Six seven eight nine ten,
The coppers let him go, again!

Why did they let him go?
'Twas his Human Rights, you know.
Which one did he cite?
The 'Fuck Off' one, and that's his Right!

~~oOo~~

Ride a Cock Horse

Ride a cock horse
To Banbury Cross
And see a fine lady,
Near naked, of course!

With bells in her nipples;
A ring through her nose;
She dingles her dangles
Where ever she goes!

~~oOo~~

The Walrus and the Carpenter

The lights were burning in the Court,
Burning for all to see.
They did their very best, it's thought,
To try and guarantee
A little cheer. It came to naught!
And none would disagree.

The heat was trying manfully
To raise the chilly gloom.
The boiler, old, by slow degree
Its fossil fuel consume;
And yet it failed, unhappily,
To warm the smallest room.

The Magistrates, so full of guile,
Were bored, as bored can be.
The only time, a hint of smile,
Was when they stopped for tea;
Or when they left, just for a while,
To nip out for a pee!

The Walrus and Carpenter
Were talking, close at hand.
They pondered how they'd blunt and blur
The Prosecution hand.
And how they further fees incur?
Or holidays they planned!

"If seven raids, by seven cops,
Nicked them for half a year;
Do you suppose," the Walrus stops,
"They'd get the Courtrooms clear?"
"I hope not," then, a tear he mops,
"Our cash would disappear!"

"Oh, felons! Will you talk to us?"
The Walrus did beseech.
"About the fight, fracas or fuss
And Bail you chose to breach?
Your alibi, we'll then discuss;
Your innocence we'll preach!"

Then four young scoundrels, hurried up,
All eager for a scrap;
With grotty jeans, a gruesome shade;
Each wore a baseball cap.
All knew their 'rights', with 'Legal Aid',
And " 'ere! I'll take no crap!"

And then four more, both small and vast,
With yet another four.
Then quick and fast, they came at last,
And more and more and more.
All shrugging off their dodgy past,
To stand before the Law.

The Carpenter sat down and thought,
He liked to think things through,
Of all the times he'd spent in Court?
He didn't have a clue!
(And yet, somehow, he seemed to know
How much he'd earned – from who!)

"It seems a shame, with all this glut,
To play them such a trick.
In spite of all we stomp and strut,
They'll end up in the Nick."
The Carpenter said nothing but;
"Their brains are very thick!"

"The time has come," the Walrus said,
"To make it very plain.
A 'guilty plea' is what I dread,
In fact, it's quite a pain!
Adjourn! Adjourn! Get in your head,
Is what we must attain.

And when, at last, upon my feet,
I'll talk of many things:
Of laws, that now are obsolete,
Entwined in legal strings.
Or how a phrase must never cheat,
Nor eloquence take wings!"

"But wait a bit!" The felons cried,
    "Before we have our chat,
We do not want to go 'inside';
    That's not our habitat."
"Oh! Have no fear," he then replied.
    They thanked him much for that.

"Your Worships, will you bear with us?"
    His waffle had begun.
"I will explore, at length discuss,
    The wrongs they may have done …
You'll surely overlook this fuss
    And won't curtail their fun?"

The magistrates thought "What a bore,
    This homily, homespun;
In fact, they'd heard it all before,
    With patience, overrun."
And so to end their dreary chore,
    Imprisoned – every one!

~~oOo~~

Ladybird

Ladybird, ladybird,
Fly away home.
You shouldn't be here;
It's too far to roam.

Go back and look after
Your spotted coxcomb!
And don't be beguiled
By that horror – "the Dome".

It sits there forlornly,
In sad monochrome.
A tawdry example
Of Hubris Syndrome!

Ladybird, ladybird,
Fly away home.
Let us be bedazzled
By glitter and chrome.

~~oOo~~

A Man

A man, on a bicycle,
Once asked me:
"How many buttercups
Live in a tree?"

I gave him the answer,
Quick as a flash.
"As many bright builders
Do it for cash!"

~~oOo~~

Justice

I stand here, you see,
Your Worships, all three,
We know that I'm guilty, it's true!
I'm sue you'll agree,
With my pedigree,
It's certainly 'time' that I'll do.

A Brief, I will see,
Who'll alter my plea;
Then get Legal Aid – what a *coup!*
The Crown Court, 'twill be,
This lawyer and me.
A Jury? They won't have a clue!

All humble, I'll be
(With no repartee!)
But oodles of deference due.
And when I am free,
As surely I'll be,
I'll blow a sweet raspberry at you!

~~oOo~~

Jack Spratt

Jack Spratt could eat no fat.
His wife could eat no lean ......

...... and so, God help us, think of that;
They're 'vegans' now – and keen!

Bye, Baby Bunting

Bye, baby bunting,
Daddy's gone a'hunting.

Any Anti in his way
Will end up futting grunting!

~~oOo~~

Twinkle Twinkle

Twinkle, twinkle little star;
How I wonder what you are?
Are you just a satellite
That beams back telly, through the night?

But then, again, you maybe not
A friendly, twinkling little dot?
Perhaps, I wonder, could it be
You're photographing shots of me?

~~oOo~~

Tweedle-dee and Tweedle-dum

Now Tweedle-dee and Tweedle-dum
Resolved to have a battle.
Said Tweedle-dee "Oi! Tweedle-dum,
You've nicked my bloody rattle!"

A passer-by, out to annoy,
Had heard them disagree.
"I'm deeply shocked, you naughty boy!"
She said, with pious glee.

Then Tweedle-dee, in terms quite stark,
Soon heard from the police
That he must face, for his remark,
A Justice of the Peace.

The weasel words, her meaning gleaned,
Were total, utter bosh!
In fact, her accusation seemed
Just sanctimonious tosh!

"I could not fail, I could not miss,
A man so vile abused.
A deeply seated prejudice
And "dumb" the word he used!"

"Outrageous!" said the worthy Beak,
"Foul language, we must stop.
It's now OK to be a sneak
And proper to eavesdrop!"

So Tweedle-dee was sent away,
Locked up for twenty years.
He begged release, to end his stay,
By shedding many tears.

When free at last and undeterred,
He sallied into battle.
"Oi! Tweedle-THICK, I want a word!
Now! Where's my bloody rattle?"

~~oOo~~

LOST: Cricket Nets

I know I put the nets away.
Much more, I'll guarantee
That all were tied up, neat, with string
And packed away, until the spring.
For Heaven's sake, where can they be?

I've asked around, both far and near.
In fact, you must agree
That not a stone is left unturned.
I'm really getting quite concerned.
A future grim, I now foresee.

Has anybody seen my nets?
The ones rolled up, by me.
The binding, strong; the knots are tight;
I hid them safely out of sight.
And so, I plea, on bended knee,

WHO'S GOT MY BLEEDING NETS?

~~oOo~~

Three Blind Mice

Three 'challenged' mice,
Three 'challenged' mice;
See how they run.
See how they run.

They all brought a case
'Gainst the farmer's wife,
Who'd "abused" their tails
With a carving knife.

She's now in jug,
For the rest of her life.
'Twas Animal Rights
That triggered her strife.

And three smug mice!
Three smug mice!

~~oOo~~

Jack Be Nimble

Jack be nimble,
Jack be quick.
For doing deals,
You're in the nick.

Since getting caught
Gets on their wick,
The Magistrates
Will give you stick.

But have no fear,
You're work is slick
And prison screws
Are pretty thick!

~~oOo~~

Half a Pound

Half a pound of roll-your own.
Or else a pack of twenty.
It's got to be the nicotine;
I'm always needing plenty!

Up and down the City Road,
We stand out here, together.
So stuff the lot of you inside
And sod the bloody weather!

~~oOo~~

To Market

To market, to market,
To buy a fat pig;
A flagon of cider,
Good for a swig.

We'll meet on the street,
A bit of a gig.
Then shout and we'll swear.
We don't give a fig!

~~oOo~~

There Was a Crooked Man

There was a crooked man
And he walked a crooked mile.
He found a crooked sixpence,
Upon a crooked stile.

That nosey Weights and Measures squad
Removed his happy smile.
They used their crooked practices
To confiscate his pile.

"What's wrong with 'quid' or 'half a crown'
That served our Treasured Isle?
All swept away by foreigners,
With beaurocratic bile."

"I love our good old measurements,
Robust and versatile.
I loathe this measly metric junk,
In good old British style!"

~~oOo~~

Eeny, Meeny

Eeny, Meeny,
Miney, Moe.
Catch an 'oopsie'
By the toe.

If he hollers,
Let him go.
Race Relations
Then won't know!

~~oOo~~

I Had a Little Nut Tree

I had a little nut tree;
Nothing would it bear.
Yet all those far off city folk
Were keen to interfere.

The 'King of Self Importance'
Came to visit me.
His pamphlets, from the Ministry,
He dolloped out – quite free!

With graphic exhortations,
To pull my finger out;
Went on to whisper in my ear,
"It's me what's got the clout!"

"Now go and be creative.
Plant something on the banks.
So others see your handiwork –
But don't expect their thanks!"

I said, "I hate your wild flowers:
(Another name for weeds.)
I will not harbour ragwort,
Nor scatter poppy seeds."

"So! Take your crummy books away,
All written by your friends
And stuff your facile focus groups
Who talk of eco-trends."

"It's me who'll help my nut tree.
With time and patience, stealth,
I'll solve its little problem
And bring it back to health."

~~oOo~~

Oh! When

Oh! When I was a little boy,
My Mother kept me in.
Her love for me, a real joy,
Was deep and genuine.

But now I'm grown. I'm fit and strong,
I've joined the teenage dross.
So! Do I care for right and wrong?
I couldn't give a toss!

~~oOo~~

Sing a Song of Sixpence

Sing a song for sixpence
And call it modern 'pop'.
You'll try and give as much offence,
By quoting agitprop.

You'll howl it out, in gibberish,
And strut about the scene.
Now! Isn't that a dainty dish
To set before the Queen?

~~oOo~~

THE PURSUIT OF
HAPPINESS …

Solomon Grundy

Solomon Grundy, Solomon Grundy,
Sniffer of glue, when offered, on Monday;
The Tuesday was hash, a whopping great spliff;
On Wednesday took coke, a generous sniff.

For Thursday some crack, the dodgiest brand,
And Friday's dope needle was quite second-hand.
When Saturday came, a massive O.D.
By Sunday 'twas ended, this hedonist spree.

In spite of the stuff, that came from a packet,
Right up to the end, he thought he could hack it!

~~oOo~~

Tom Tom

Tom, Tom, the Piper's son,
Stole a pig, and was on the run.
He'd come from jail;
Released on Bail.
He stole another,
Just for fun!

Little Bo Peep

Little Bo Peep has mislaid her sheep
And doesn't know where to find them.
For during her sleep, they escaped from the keep.
A left open gate is her problem.

The ramblers, all keen, have been on the scene
And claiming their new "Right to Roam."
They like to be seen in booties, all green,
And striding out far from their home.

They dress, for the day, the usual way,
In clothes of an eye-catching hue.
No thought, as they stray, that some of us may
Prefer a more camouflaged view!

Of course, they will moan, of paths overgrown
With bracken, a thistle or weed.
"Why can't it be sown, with grass that is mown,
On which the sweet bunnies can feed?"

Our Little Bo Peep, the route she must keep
All trim, in a manicured way.
The leaves she must sweep and pile in a heap;
Not scattered in some disarray.

Old 'fridges and cans; some burnt-out old vans;
Pink wrappers, all sprinkled with glitter;
The junk of the clans; detritus of fans;
All day she must clean up the litter.

Her trustworthy friend will then have to mend
A hasp or a broken down fence.
The cost, to attend, is cash, without end
And all without due recompense.

She asks, "Is it fair, this rural affair,
Be settled by those from the cities?
About my welfare, they really don't care.
It bloody well gets on my titties!"

~~oOo~~

The Queen of Hearts

The King of Hearts,
His journey starts,
All on a summer's day.
When he departs
From his ramparts,
The Court comes out to play!

The Queen of Hearts
Parades her tarts,
Inviting all to stay.
Well schooled in arts,
She there imparts
Some games, both straight – and gay!

The Knave of Hearts
Lures fat old farts
To sample – and to pay!
Then, from the tarts,
Their cash he carts
And salts it all away!

~~oOo~~

Ring-a-ring o' Roses

Ring-a-ring o' roses,
A pocket full of posies.

Take a whiff,
A whopping sniff,
To ward off halitosis!

~~oOo~~

Mary Had a Little Lamb

Mary had a little lamb,
Its fleece was white as snow.
She got it with an E.U. scam,
In subsidies, you know.

A friend had said, "This hand-me-down.
You always claim the most!"
She sent the form to Brussels Town.
Her cheque came in the post!

~~oOo~~

A Green Christmas

Christmas is a'coming;
The geese are getting fat.
And do you think they're for the pot?
You're getting none of that!

Now go and pick some broccoli,
Or brussels sprouts will do.
That's all there is for Christmas nosh,
And God bless you!

~~oOo~~

Ennui

I think I may be getting bored;
You know the sort of thing?
The amble through an empty room,
All cold and grey and filled with gloom,
That seeps into the panelling
And sits there, safely stored.

I feel as if I'm nearly bored,
Where indolence will cling.
The languid lying on a couch
The soggy pose, the droopy slouch.
I cannot make my motors sing,
Nor strike an active chord.

I'm pretty sure I'm getting bored;
It's not so comforting.
The papers, read, are on the floor;
I cannot face another chore;
A challenge new, so gruelling.
Will bring me scant reward.

And now I know I'm almost bored.
I simply cannot bring
Myself to skip, nor prance, nor talk,
Nor potter for a country walk.
An energetic Highland fling
Is, oh! So untoward!

Life's such a drag. So help me Lord
To get my thoughts to zing.
I'm comatose, all half asleep,
Enough to make a strong man weep.
No more will aspirations wing.
You're right! I'm very bored.

~~oOo~~

Fee Fi Fo Fum

Fee Fi Fo Fum,
I smell the blood
Of an English man.

Cut the skin,
The gore is thin
And flows much like a lager can!

~~oOo~~

Round and Round the Garden

Round and round the garden,
With a teddy bear!

One step. Two step.
Doo-lally, now, I hear.

It's So Easy

When I was a lad and still at school,
My colleagues called me a simple fool.
I played no sport, I played no games.
What's more they called me nasty names.
They made my life such a misery,
I determined to become a Labour M.P.

I did no work, I joined no firm.
I lived off the dole for quite a term.
And during this time, with the midnight oil,
To rallies I went, with a diligent toil.
I lived 'by the book', so assiduously,
I was sure to become a Labour M.P.

I then sought out, in a move quite bold
A Union boss, decrepit and old.
A man who'd moaned, for most of his life,
Who'd climbed to the top, with toil and strife,
That dinosaur, most utterly,
Was my stepping-stone as a Labour M.P.

His son-in-law and uncle, too,
With brothers and sisters and retinue,
Would mix the votes and muddle the cash;
Then salt their loot in a slush fund stash.
This then ensured their constituency
Would always return a Labour M.P.

I got their nod at Election time,
Like a walk on part, in a pantomime.
I shook some hands and a baby kissed;
I even was seen with a Communist.
The Union vote was a guarantee,
They elected me a Labour M.P.

And so I strode into Parliament,
Where 'paid up' folk had me kindly sent.
On a very back bench, I took my place,
Where Ministers, proud, could see my face.
I nodded with awe – and frequently,
Till I soon became a model M.P.

As time went by, and my locks turned grey,
I learnt how to say what I'm told to say.
I'd ask all the questions they'd ask me to,
Then kept very quiet, as I always do!
I stated their views, so obsequiously,
That now I'm a Lord and not an M.P.

****

So listen all, who ever you may be,
If you want to rise to the top of the tree,
Stick fast to your vows, with this golden rule:
(And raise two fingers at your chums from school!)
Just oil your way through a Union, like me
And you could become a Labour M.P.

~~oOo~~

Old Mother Hubbard

Old Mother Hubbard
Went to the cupboard,
To fetch her dear doggie a bone.

The dog liked to eat
Great dollops of meat;
So scarpered – and left the old crone!

~~oOo~~

Old King Cole

Old King Cole
Was a merry old soul;
But a spaced out sort, was he!

He called for his pipe
(The small, illegal type!)
Then handed round the ding-dong – free!

He sniffed a bit of this,
And he smoked a bit of that,
And he swallowed some little pills, too!

His only trouble was
He soon got bust, because
His Parking Fines were overdue!

~~oOo~~

Boys and Girls

"Boys and girls come out to play,
The moon is shining, bright as day.
Bring your sticks and bring your stones.
Come with us, to combat zones."

"Smash some windows; bash the boot;
Break a windscreen; take the loot.
Wreaking havoc everywhere.
Bedlam! Mayhem! We don't care!"

"Girls and boys come out to play.
The moon is shining, bright as day.
And will it cost? I cannot say.
So! What the hell! Insurers pay!"

~~oOo~~

Mary, Mary

"Mary, Mary,
Quite contrary,
How does your garden grow?"

"'Twas featured, you know,
On a gardening show.
The decking is twee and pseudo!"

~~oOo~~

P.R. Consultant's Love-song

Ms. Jo Hunter Dunn, Ms. Jo Hunter Dunn,
Varnished and tarnished by Val d'Isere sun.
The sway of your hips; the power to stun;
A promise of love and nights filled with fun.

Dazzle me, Goddess, you Queen of the Slopes,
Mistress of Moguls. Oh! Show me the ropes.
You're someone who's positive, keen and who copes.
You fill me with passion; you stimulate hopes.

You work in a Bank and own a dot.com.
I know that you trade with gusto, aplomb;
You're buying, on margin, the profits there from,
All pay for your Porsche. You're making a bomb!

I hear that you cook, with consummate ease;
You fly your own 'plane, alone, if you please.
Your place in the sun is large, Portuguese,
And far from your yacht, you windsurf the breeze.

Join me, dear Venus, 'off piste,' on a run,
Then tell me, my love, your heart have I won?
Oh! Rapturous joy. My courtship is done!
I'm going to live with Ms. Hunter Dunn.

~~oOo~~

Breeding Stock

There is a young lady, lives in a shoe;
A gaggle of kids, her polyglot crew.
She has many lovers, all in a queue,
Who patiently wait their turn to yahoo!

Now Family Planning, long overdue;
Our heroine, here, just hasn't a clue!
So! Won't someone please, explain what to do:
She mustn't say yes – but try "toodle-oo".

~~oOo~~

Speak Firmly

Speak firmly to your little boy
And beat him, when he sneezes.
For many years that was the norm;
A wallop, when he teases.

But now-a-days, that's not allowed.
It's cuddles, hugs and squeezes.
No ticking off, no stern rebuke.
He does just what he pleases!

The Pest

The invitation came by 'phone,
Delivered in stentorian tone.
"For God's sake, get here double quick
My favoured guests have cried off sick."

Her house was cold and none too clean;
Our welcome host was nowhere seen
Save, calling through the kitchen door,
"The drinky-poos are in the store."

We then, amongst filthy pans,
Ate processed peas from Asda cans.
The chicken Kiev, still quite raw,
Had come from Marks and Spencer's store.

Her wine was like some sweaty socks,
Antipodean, from a box.
And in the butter, frozen hard,
The budgerigar had left his card.

Next day she burnt the breakfast toast;
Her dog then took the Sunday roast.
And as we left, above the din,
Heard "Shit! You've finished all my gin!"

~~oOo~~

The Best

The invitation, from our host,
Came clearly written, in the post.
It stated time and mode of dress,
And sweetly begged us, "Please say yes."

Her house was warm. The table laid.
The dinner cooked. (She had no maid!)
Our glasses, large were often filled
With champagne good – and not too chilled.

She introduced, with gracious ease,
The sort of guest it's nice to please.
With simple ease, with judgement fine,
She gently murmered, "Shall we dine?"

The splendid meal was *haute cuisine*,
With wines, quite rare and seldom seen.
Her coffee from a Georgian pot
Was freshly ground and piping hot.

On feathered beds, we slept till late;
A treat we did appreciate.
And when, at last, our stay was done
She thanked us all. "It has been fun."

~~oOo~~

St Ives

When I was staying in St Ives,
I met a man with seven wives.
And since the ladies seemed content,
I offered him a compliment.

"Well done, old chap! You must be proud
To be so lavishly endowed!
And do you service all their needs?"
"Oh no," he cried, "I live in Leeds!"

~~oOo~~

Father William

"You are old, Father William," the young man said.
"And your hair has become very white;
And yet you incessantly teach little boys.
Do you think, at your age, it is right?"

"In my youth," Father William replied, with a scowl,
"I gave my affections to God.
I find your presumptions utterly vile,
You sour and impertinent sod!"

"I've heard all the gossip. The rumours are rife.
I'll shame you, I certainly can!
What's more" said the youth, with a self-righteous smirk,
"I think you're a dirty old man!"

"I don't give a toss," Father William declared,
"When you talk of some juvenile 'frolics'.
Unless you piss off, you'll very soon get
A bloody good boot, in the bollocks!"

~~oOo~~

Little Miss Muffet

Little Miss Muffett
Sits on her tuffet
And beams at you
One of her smiles.

But unknown to you,
The picture ain't true.
She's rickets
And suffers from piles!

Professional Foul

The Agent for my little firm
is idle, through and through.
His fuel injected Audi car
is deep metallic blue.
He always sports a Burberry scarf
And wears green wellies, too!

My Lawyer's car, a Jaguar,
is slim; a slippery marque.
He seldom ventures near the Law;
(the work's done by his clerk!)
And yet he charges 'Partners Rates,'
The avaricious shark.

My Broker's Merc is spanking new;
it takes his fishing rod.
He, as of right, once gently slipped
in shoes, his father trod.
All pomp and circumstance, he struts.
A self appointed God.

My Builder's car is also new,
a large Range Rover truck.
He says he made an honest pile
by hauling loads of muck.
He knows I know that isn't true!
My home's the gold he's struck.

Accountant's BMWs
have litres, by the score;
With quadraphonic gadgetry
and Wilton, on the floor.
Mine has a wretched monogram
emblazoned on his door!

And now a new and added blight,
my Landscape Architect,
Who drives a massive 4x4
to visit and inspect.
She tramples round – and then she shouts;
"These woods – you must protect!"

I used to run a little car,
a Morris 1000 van.
It was an old and trusted friend;
it ran and ran and ran.
But years gone by, it had to go
when 'pay up' time began.

And in my muddled, simple way
I somehow fail to see
Just why it's right they huff and puff
and then they charge a fee?
Their jobs are there, to make ME rich?
I want a car – for ME!

~~oOo~~

Marriage *à la Mode*

They meet and chat and then they dine.
A thigh is gently squeezed.
Their conversation flows with wine.
A fleeting glance is seized.

And when the couples re-align,
A rendezvous is teased.
The husbands think they should entwine.
The wives are NOT so pleased!

~~oOo~~

Hostess

"Oh, darling! Do pop into Tescos
And pick up some things which I've missed.
We've got that young couple, they're vegans;
Then promise me NOT to get pissed.

We mustn't eat eggs – and no fish, dear,
Nor fillet that's trimmed from the bone.
It's French beans, all flown in from Kenya;
They say they're 'organically' grown.

Perhaps we should start with some dips, love;
Guacamole will do as a snack.
For pudding, it's got to be yoghurt
That's strained through the fleece of a yak!

They'll never touch genuine coffee;
And decaffeinated won't do.
So find me some herbal concoction
That virgins have plucked in Peru.

And what's more, don't talk about cricket;
Your rugby will have to be missed.
I do think you might make an effort.
Oh, sod it! You've gone and got pissed!"

~~oOo~~

Host

"These people who only eat lettuce,
Then nibble some nuts from a bowl
Are totally, utterly tiresome;
This 'smugger-than-thou' rigmarole.

And me? I am rather old fashioned.
These faddy foods don't pass my lips.
In fact, the one thing I fancy?
A juicy great steak – and some chips.

I like a wee nip of the whisky,
That's malt, with a small knob of ice;
And will you just make it a double.
You really can't call it a vice.

I'm partial to wine from the *Touraine*;
A dry little number will do.
Then followed by something from *Bordeaux*,
That's ancient and *Premier Cru*.

Now! Who are the creatures for dinner?
Their name, I think I have missed.
Dear God! What a dreary young couple.
Shank goodnesh, I've gone and got pished!"

~~oOo~~

Where Are You Going To?

"Where are you going to, my Pretty Maid?"
"I'm going a'milking, Sir." She said.
"This 'Quota' you have; a 'License to Trade';
All 'Registered Land', with 'Set-a-side Aid'?"

"Oh, Sir! You're a one", the Pretty Maid said.
"I've found something new that's much better paid.
It's not the old cow, I'm going to raid.
I'm milking the system, Sir!" She said.

~~oOo~~

Blood Sports

The Colonel ran his private shoot
with acumen and flair.
He liked to have his orders heard.
He liked to make them clear.
His guns were called, to gather round,
So every one could hear.

"We start the day with unwashed youths,
all dirt and sloppy dressed.
They slouch about the heart of town.
They really are a pest.
You'll spot them once the drive begins;
They cry out 'I protest!'

We'll then move on to County Hall,
To bag a clerk or two.
They're either shuffling papers round
Or standing in a queue.
Now don't be greedy. Take your pick.
We only want a few.

We'll next flush out some feminists.
(I fear no *object d'art*!)
Don't hope for gaudy plumage here,
you won't get very far.
They only wear old dungarees
and seldom any bra.

And last, before our luncheon break,
the Traffic Warden Drive.
They'll swarm at you from every side,
like bees around the hive.
All buzzing busy-bodies, they;
leave none of them alive.

When well refreshed, the repast done,
I want you all to share
In blasting off at Rent-a-mob
and those with lengthy hair.
All standing with their hand on hips
and shouting 'It's not fair!'

To end the shoot, round off our day,
the drive I most prefer.
The one that gives us real fun;
The Blood Sport Saboteur.
Go get him, lads and bring him down,
that manky, mangy cur.

There's nothing more to add, except
just one thing I must say;
I simply cannot understand
all those who rant each day.
Why can't they lead their lives – like me,
the quiet and peaceful way?"

~~oOo~~

Finale

I've huffed and I've puffed,
with nods and a wink.
I've tilted at windmills;
gone to the brink.
Berating my foes,
their glory to shrink,
So far, fingers crossed,
I've kept out of clink.

So ....

I'll lay down my pen,
the paper and ink.
I'll take off my specs
and drink up my drink.
My angst is all spent,
I've caused enough stink.
A good time to close
is now – *don't you think*?

The End

Scullion

His first job, after leaving school, was as a messenger in the dispatch department of an advertising agency. He was sacked. He then became a laundrette salesman, before being employed as a fruit machine and jukebox mechanic. For seventeen years he cleaned out the ladies loos, at an English stately home. He is now employed as a tractor driver and part time gardener's boy.

Richard Kingston

He now works out of his 'Freehand Design' studio, in Somerset. Recent commissions have included pieces of sculpture for Hamlyns (Publishers,) and a complete design package for the Aiken Drum band. Most recently, he has created 'The Tara Box,' a mini shrine and statuette, along with its fully illustrated companion book, now available from Amazon.com.

~oOo~

"NAUGHTY!"

POLITICALLY INCORRECT NURSERY VERSE

Jack and Jill

Jack chased Jill
Right up the hill
And, at the top,
He caught her!

Jill came down,
With half a crown,
For 'naughty' games
He taught her!

~~oOo~~

Published by Bunford Press
www.bunfordpress.com

Printed in the United Kingdom
by Lightning Source UK Ltd.
107386UKS00001B/85-159